Shadows on the Flats

Shadows
on the
Flats

THE SALTWATER IMAGES
OF CHET RENESON AND ED GRAY

Essays by Ed Gray
Paintings and drawings by Chet Reneson

WILLOW CREEK PRESS

Minocqua, Wisconsin

Published by WILLOW CREEK PRESS
           P.O. Box 147
           Minocqua, WI 54548

For information on other Willow Creek titles,
write or call 1-800-850-WILD

Designed by Patricia Bickner Linder

Library of Congress Cataloging-in-Publication Data:

Gray, Ed
     Shadows on the flats : the saltwater images of Chet
Reneson and Ed Gray / essays by Ed Gray : paintings and
drawings by Chet Reneson.
        p.   cm.
     ISBN 1-57223-127-0 (hc : alk. paper)
     1. Saltwater flats fly fishing—Bahamas. 2. Saltwater fly
fishing—Bahamas—Pictorial works.   I. Reneson, Chet.
II. Title.
SH578.B3G735   1997
799.1'66463—dc21   97-28062
                                                    CIP

Printed in Canada

For Bonnie & John, Dolores & Lynn, Jacquelyn & John:
It's always the 'hamas when you guys are there.

Thanks,
Ed

*T*hey live in a world of flickered mirage, in the fractal sheerings of Bahamian light dancing on bright sand in shallow water. In a place without shade, they are shadows: You see them when they are not there, and when they are, you do not.

They arrive silent as thought, hesitant, shimmering, almost invisible, for the sunlight itself seems to pass through them, cleaving itself into rippling shards that refract around the swimming fish, dissolving their individual shapes into an abstraction of the water itself.

When you do see them, always it is just a moment after you have sensed them, as if you suddenly remembered that they were here. Bonefish. Right there. Coming this way.

Shadows on the flats.

• • •

An island dream begins on first waking up. In the half light of an early tropical morning, the warm ocean itself comes into my room, lapping gently against my rising consciousness and whispering bright, rippled messages from across the shoreline and through the rustling sea grapes at the edge of the beach. Hibiscus warmth and morning glory cool ride through the jalousie slats with the rising sun, slowly eroding the lassitude of sleep, calling from outside, murmuring that this will be a day and it's already begun. Lifting with the light, I move toward the long day's fishing that lies ahead.

I have slept with images. Flitting shadows and cruising silver, liquid blue and blinding white, wind wash and salt crackle, thin horizons against the palest of skies, distant, calling and flat. On the outside wall of the cottage my fly rods rest on pegs, rigged, rinsed and ready. Down at the dock in the lagoon is a flats skiff, pinfish and juvenile snappers schooled under its shielding hull as tiny droplets of morning dew evanesce from the boat's seats and gunwales, evaporating through the growing brightness toward the certain showers of later this afternoon. Several days wading the flats are already

behind me on this trip and more lie ahead; there is no reason to hurry, and I don't.

Blanched shell fragments crackle softly in the mat of scrub pine needles under my sandals as I walk toward breakfast in the soft morning air. The wind has not yet come up and the bay water lies flat and blue all the way to a cloudless horizon. Small crabs skitter between the shaded pathway and the open beach already taking on heat with the increasing angle of the sun. A pair of sanderlings scuttle along the edges of the two-inch surflets that lap at the shore and a Cuban Emerald hummingbird darts and hovers among the bougainvilleas on the path ahead of me. Today I am going to fish alone.

On the other side of the island, through a mile-long tidal river open on both shores, is a large lagoon, edged with mangroves and small beaches and fed by a natural deep-water channel that cuts through the hard limestone that forms the outer shoreline of the island itself. All of the water in the lagoon comes in and out with the tidal flux,

flooding and ebbing through the natural channel like a reversing river, draining and refilling the mile-wide lake with three feet of new water twice every day. And with the incoming tide come the searching flats-feeders: barracuda, bonefish and, sometimes, permit.

It is a place that had been shown to me years before, on my first trip to the island, by a Bahamian guide named Roland who didn't usually fish it.

"Too shahlow, mon," he had explained. "Get the boat stuck up in thaht place, be a long walk out."

But a long walk was exactly what I did want, then and, even more, today. I hadn't been able to convince Roland, back on that first time, that I really would rather walk than ride, even if it meant seeing far fewer fish during the course of a day. Standing in the bow of a flats skiff well poled, gliding without effort on your part over water that is sometimes too deep to wade in, is by far the most effective way to cover a large flat. From that height you can see fish in the water well before they are in casting range. And the casting is easier, too: Your back cast stays higher above the water and the shooting line lies dry and coiled at your feet, frictionless, ready to fly. But the tradeoff is that you spend only half your time up there, in the bow, searching, ready to cast; the rest of the day you spend sitting down, out of the way while your fishing partner takes a turn up front. So the boat has to produce twice as many opportunities in order to break even with a lone angler wading.

One answer, of course, is to hire the boat and the guide just for yourself, but not many can afford to do that even when it's possible. A good flats guide is a lot rarer than a rich fisherman and most island resorts won't allow monopolization. So you ride with a partner, fishing half the time, or you get out and walk, something I learned to do the first time I ever went bonefishing. It's been my preference ever since.

More than a preference now, and breaking

even has nothing to do with it. For I have come to love not just the fish and the fishing, but the islands themselves. As tangible places and private metaphors, these sun-washed limestone-and-coral archipelagoes rising thin, white and green from the indigo depths and ultramarine distances of the Atlantic Ocean have captured a part of me that wants always to be anchored to them, both physically and spiritually. I want to walk on them, even when I'm beyond their shores, so I get out of the boat whenever it's possible. No island ceases at the water's edge when you wade on its flats, and when you walk on your own two feet, hunting in its shallows, no ocean calls you alien. Here, in this delicately-overlapping zone of air and water, where predatory and wary fish ride in on a veneer of ocean to hunt just inches above the flooded land on which you walk, hunting them, there is a symmetry of common existence unlike any that I have found yet, either in the wild or, after half a lifetime of searching, in the arts. A symmetry that

calls me now toward the unnamed lagoon where I will walk alone for all of this day, seeking shadows and finding light, casting toward images with lives of their own, hunting in common for something that already surrounds us both.

The sun is lifting. Breakfast coffee and sweet rolls call from the kitchen just ahead of me on this island pathway along the beach, but already I am past them in my mind. Well before it's started, I'm already fishing.

efore I discovered that the catalog companies were marketing neoprene diver's booties as flats wading shoes, I used to wear an old pair of running shoes while bonefishing. They worked poorly, shielding the soles of my feet from the deeper punctures of broken coral and fractured conch shells but trapping so much sand and sharpened bits of bottom detritus inside the shoes themselves that after the first day of fishing the skin of both my feet would have been abraded and blistered past annoyance and well toward torment. Pulling on those wet, sandy sneakers each day thereafter and then stepping into salt water was painful enough on some mornings to keep me in the boat for an hour or more before the psychic discomfort of being there instead of out on the flats, walking, where I knew I should be, would begin to outweigh the burning red chafing that I could feel well before my feet went over the side and into the brine.

Those days are over. Today, slipping painlessly into the nylon-lined comfort of a good, well-fitted pair of flats booties, zipping them snug and tight against my ankles and stepping almost without sensation into knee-deep water over a hardened mix of old coral, granular sand and rasping turtle grass, gives me the reciprocal of the sense I get at home in the deep of winter, stepping outside in my felt-lined Sorels into snow so cold that it squeaks under my weight as I walk through it, feeling none of its sub-zero chill. Feeling, in fact and at least in my feet, almost nothing at all.

This past winter I told my son, Will, as we walked through a new snowfall with the dogs scampering and bounding ahead of us, that animals must not feel the sensation of cold the way we do, external and immediate, instantly reacting to it as we would a cut or a burn. Instead, I theorized, the lack of heat must slowly work against their whole systems, dissipating energy and causing discomfort but not direct pain. So when we walk out here in the snow like this, I went on, wearing thick boots and insulated jackets, we get a small chance to sense the winter the way an animal that lives in it senses it, walking in deep snow without any

immediate discomfort but needing to keep moving in order to prevent the cold from seeping into the cores of our bodies.

A similar connection, I've come to realize, occurs here in the warm Bahamian flats, where the crustacean-seeking bonefish and permit grub routinely among hardened particles that would cut and bruise the soles of my feet, using their mouths to do the digging. Obviously it doesn't hurt them to move through the sharpened grit, and when I wear the flats booties, it doesn't hurt me either. For us both, this part of the flats environment is thus moved into the background, a thing to be aware and mildly careful of, but not something that intrudes to the top of your consciousness with constant painful and injurious reminders of where you are.

But of course you do feel it. The bottom is there, underfoot, sometimes smooth, sometimes hard, often so soft that you sink into it well above your ankles, and occasionally jagged and sharp

where the coral is newer or the limestone harder and less eroded. These are the continuing messages of place needed by a well-centered hunter, and none are apparent to an angler riding above them in a poled skiff.

This morning, as the fiberglass skiff comes down from its high-speed plane to settle and drift while Roland shuts off the big Yamaha outboard and reaches for his boat pole, I'm eager for exactly those messages from precisely this place. Ahead of us in the mangroves is the channel leading to the lagoon where I plan to spend the day alone while Roland and Becky ghost off down the shoreline to the poling flats where they'll fish. There's very little wind and already the day has become hot.

"May be all right today," says Roland as he begins poling toward the channel. "The wind down."

"Will it stay down?" I ask.

"You cahn never tell, but may-be for some while," he answers. I turn and grin at Becky. This is as unequivocal as Roland ever gets and we both know it. No Bahamian speaks of the weather in absolutes; today will be a beauty.

"Are you sure this is what you want to do?" asks Becky as Roland begins to pole us through the channel itself. "We can come back in an hour."

"No," I say, giving her the answer she already knows. "Only if something changes with you two. I've been looking forward to this for a long time."

And I have. It takes several trips to a guided fishing resort before they will let you do something that breaks their standard pattern, especially if it means being left alone without one of their guides for any time at all. But with familiarity can come trust, and it has taken me a couple of years to get to this point with Roland and with his employers. My day alone in the lagoon has been a while coming, but it is here. The skiff slides soundlessly out of the mangrove channel and into the lagoon.

Here is where I will spend this day, in a sparkling place without edges. In the absence of

wind, with no surface ripple to catch the morning sun, the water is almost invisible; we seem to ride on air, inches above the white sand bottom. Across the lagoon, almost a mile away, the dark line of mangroves rides like a mirage, heat-wobbled but in perfect focus under an azurine bowl of sky. It is a universe of clarity, and it is mine for the rest of the day.

•   •   •

More than for any other reason, I go to wild places to find silences, the kind that you find only there and that you cannot find even in those places unless you have been away from them. For no natural place is ever actually silent; it's the quiet in your own head that you seek, and it takes some time before you begin to hear it. First you have to let the cacophony that you brought with you drain away, clattering off sporadically toward the horizon. And the farther the horizon, the quieter, finally, it can get.

Here in the lagoon the silence presents itself slowly, waiting for the outboard to drone steadily down the coast and around the bend of the island, a sound that I know from experience will be physically gone well before it seems that way to me.

But finally it does, and I begin slowly to look around. In my hands are two fly rods still in their aluminum tubes and on my back is a small green daypack, packed with lunch, water, sunscreen, a raincoat, some Tarponwear pants, a camera,

lightweight binoculars, two fly reels, three spools of leader material and a couple of plastic boxes of flies; I'm prepared to wear the pack while I fish, but it would be better to set it down someplace. A hundred yards to my left is a sandy spit of harder ground with beach grasses growing above the flotsam and dried seaweed that marks the high tide line. It's a good place to put it, and I start that way, sliding my feet quietly through the warm, knee-deep water, trying to make no disturbance even though I haven't yet strung up a rod.

The bottom here is bright white, sandy and hard, with small patches of turtle grass mixed in, colonizing their way ahead of the larger, ten-acre swath of it that I can see fifty yards to my left, sloping away toward deeper, greener water. There will be fish there for sure; if not now, then surely at some time today.

As I get closer to the dry sand spit, and as the water gets shallower — now at mid-calf and much warmer — an eight-inch barracuda darts out of my path, shooting ten feet in a flickering little blur before stopping instantly to turn and face me.

"Who are you kidding?" I say to the little 'cuda. "I've got flies in here bigger than you."

In fact I do. Deep in the daypack that I'm about to shed are a couple of barracuda flies nine inches long, sparse green streamers with a bit of flash tied into them, designed to imitate the needlefish that no barracuda will refuse if you can make it move fast enough through the water. Which is something I plan to do today; it's why I brought the second fly rod.

Up on the beach I happily take off the daypack, letting the dry Bahamian air work against the clammy shirt and hot sweat on my back where the pack had pressed. Leaving the pack on the sand I turn to scan the lagoon through my polaroids. My standpoint is now three feet above the water's surface instead of two under it, and the slight increase in elevation has revealed several orders of magnitude more bottom than I could see from the lower position, standing in the water. Later in the day, with the sun higher and their resultant shadows more sharply delineated, I'll be able to see moving bonefish for hundreds of yards from here; even now, I'm certain that I'd see them if they were already in this part of the lagoon. Intently I scan the water, looking past the surface and down to the variegated bottom. Nothing. It's disappointing; I really do want them to be here.

Well, what would you do if you saw one? I ask myself. Hit it with a rod tube?

Right, I answer. Good thought.

Stringing up the rods, I try to halt this conversation I'm having with myself, a lifetime habit that's hard to break. But if I'm to get anywhere near the sort of natural silence that I came here to seek, this talking has got to stop. What's the difference whether you hear it first through your ears or not? Chatter is chatter, and its specific words echo for a long time in a mind that uses them almost exclusively to order its thoughts.

But ordering thoughts is just what I came here to avoid today, here in this clear lagoon absent of people. What I want is for the images of this place to come to me in their own sequence, and I want to clear my mind so that I can react to them naturally, whatever that means. And just what does that mean, here to me, today in this place? I'm not sure. Spontaneously, I suppose. Without language if possible. Removed from the ticking increments of measured time. And definitely somewhere distant from this question-and-answer format.

This isn't going to be easy, I tell myself as I pull the line and leader through the tip guide of the second rod, and it won't happen in the first few minutes. No it won't, I sneer at myself. You're still measuring with those ticking increments.

Oh yeah, I answer. You're right.

•   •   •

Selecting a bonefish fly has become more difficult for me as time has gone by. In the first few years that Becky and I traveled to the Bahamas, specifically to Deep Water Cay on the East End of Grand Bahama Island, I followed Brad Jackson's advice as if he were there with us, whispering over my shoulder to just tie on a hot pink Mini Puff and don't worry about it.

"Three-part leaders tapered down to ten pounds, triple surgeon's knots and the hot head," he'd told me over the phone from The Fly Shop in California when he heard we were going to Deep

Water. "It's all you need. Four-inch strips till you feel the fish pick up the fly, then one long steady strip till he feels the hook, lift as he turns to run, hit him once and hang on."

It worked like a dream. Not one bonefish refused the Mini Puff all week, and Becky and I both spent a lot of time hanging on. At the end of the trip I gave a dozen unused flies to our guide Leroy, and watched as he carefully separated out the four remaining hot heads, holding them in his hand while he put the other patterns into the old tackle box he used for his clients who showed up without flies. Leroy then carefully put the Mini Puffs in his shirt pocket, looking up just in time to see the quizzical look on my face.

"Use these for myself," he said, patting his shirt and letting a little smile accent the thank-you he had already said when I first handed them to him.

For about two years after that first trip, I rarely fished with another tie. But gradually the effectiveness of the hot head seemed to diminish, and I have no idea why. As a caster I was getting better; my presentations were more consistent to feeding fish, and I know the bonefish could see the fly. Most of the time they would turn on it, scuttling and darting over the bottom the way they do just before a take, but sometimes they would then simply turn away. So, feeling lost and somewhat befuddled, I began changing flies largely at random. Of course, I then hooked fish largely at random.

Now I'm very much at random when it comes to deciding what to tie on. Dull brown seems to work consistently, especially when it's overcast, and I've had some success with a Lime Candy fly, a bright green Lee Wulff invention that I like to toss at barracuda if there are no bones around. Sometimes when they are around; I like barracuda, as undistracted a life-force as any on the planet. Commitment is a word redefined for you the first time you watch one of them decide to eat something.

Thinking about that, and remembering the little 'cuda just off the beach, decides it for me. I take out a Lime Candy and tie it on the end of my leader — three parts down to ten pounds, triple surgeon's knots, as always. That much still holds true, Brad. Literally.

And so, rigged, ready and finally alone on the edge of the quieting lagoon of clarity, it's time to walk into it. It's time to begin the fishing itself.

• • •

There are essentially two types of hunting. In one the prey is hiding somewhere and you must go out and find it, and in the other the prey is moving and you must try to intercept it. Bonefish are an almost perfect sporting quarry: they never stop moving, and they stay hidden while they go.

They stay hidden because of their natural camouflage — a combination of coloration and reflectivity that distorts the passage of light as it strikes them, mimicking those same attributes of the water in which they live — and because of their ability to move in very shallow water without breaking the surface tension just inches above them as they swim. You have to learn not just how to see them, but how to know it when you have. No one does this quickly.

A good place to start is on a shallow flat with a light bottom, preferably one that is all sand, or at least mostly so, the kind of shallows that invites a shell-seeker to wade barefoot out from a hot beach. Bonefish will come into these bright flats routinely

and without fear if small crabs and shrimps are abundant enough, and when they do, they cast crisp shadows just beneath themselves. I like to begin the day on a flat like this if I can, because it takes me some time to develop the sort of thought-blocking intensity that hunting them over more difficult bottoms requires. Here, while my mind still retains the gyring distractions of the night before, I'm less likely to misapprehend a pod of bonefish as it swims toward me, hunting. At a distance of 75 yards or so, they'll look like tadpoles against the white sand bottom, tapered like teardrops and almost black.

Just like the ones right here, in front of me.

Damn it. Here they come. I haven't even pulled line off the reel yet, haven't made a warm-up cast, haven't done anything.

Sweeping the rod sidearm and low to the water so they won't see anything, I frantically yank line out from the reel as I work it out with shooting little false casts until at least the heavy forward taper of the seven-weight floating line is out beyond the tip top. My eyes are on the fish, moving steadily down the shoreline toward me. Six, maybe eight of them. I strip 30 or 40 more feet of line off the reel, letting it drop in coils onto the water in front of my knees.

What I want to do is to get the fly out and in the water just ahead of their swimming path, dropping it quietly onto the surface in time for it to sink the eighteen inches to the bottom in front of the bonefish just before they get there. That way I can begin to retrieve it in Brad's four-inch strips as soon as they can see it, making it look to the fish like a scuttling little . . . Lime Candy. Damn again. Before it's even in the air for the first time, I have my doubts about using this fly. A barracuda-compatible compromise seems chicken-hearted and too tentative now. Dull brown would be better. Way better.

Even the Mini Puff.

Here they come. Time for one cast, maybe.

I roll-cast forward to get some line out in front of the rod and then backcast and lift, shooting as much as I can out high and behind me before leaning into one forward cast to measure the distance. The fly line uncoils itself out and over the water, toward the bonefish, straightening fully and hanging there, four feet above the surface for just an instant before I haul it sharply back and then shoot it forward one more time. The line uncoils with the fly seeming to follow it through the air, a dark blur like a speeding insect that suddenly dives onto the water twenty feet in front of the pod. They don't spook. The fly sinks.

When the fish are ten feet from where the fly landed, I begin to move it, stripping in line with just the movement of my left wrist. You can't see the fly on the bottom that far away; I just imagine it being pulled along the sand by its hopefully invisible leader, leaving a little trail of disturbed sand as it skitters along in front of the hungry bonefish.

One of them turns sharply, accelerates, followed immediately by two more. With their snouts right on the bottom, the three fish dart this way and that, hunting and competitive as wild dogs. Continuing the short strips, I try to keep the fly moving steadily, try to keep myself calm. The fish seem to be right on top of the fly, quickening, and then there is resistance on the line, a gathering heaviness like weed-fouling, but there are no weeds on this sand flat. Without lifting the rod I pull steadily back on the line with my left arm, tightening against the weight which suddenly pulls back against me. Sharply I lift the rod tip and strike the fish with one short, hard tug on the line.

Down goes the fly rod, arcing spastically against my effort to keep it up. The fly line is yanked forcefully from the loose grip of my left hand as the entire length of it from the rod tip to where the bonefish struck comes up and out of the water in a taughtening flash of thrown water as the bonefish turns against the leader and bolts

directly away from the beach, scattering its pod-mates like exploded ghosts. All the slack fly line at my feet flies up and away, rattling and stinging through the cupped fingers of my left hand as I try to keep it from bunching and slamming into the stripping guide of the rod all at once. I hold my breath — this is where most of them are lost — until the last of the loose line shoots up into the rod guides, snapping taut against the reel spool and yanking it into an instant loud whine of high-speed revolution.

At the first pull of the drag, the bonefish seems to accelerate, arcing away with undiminished speed as I watch the end of the fly line flash up and out of the reel, followed seamlessly by the yellow Micron backing now humming from the reel arbor. The bonefish has sprinted fifty feet in a couple of seconds and is now moving even faster, cutting away from me at a progressively more acute angle, dragging the tightened fly line like a cheesecutter's wire sideways through the water, loudly ripping the surface like a torn bed sheet behind the speeding bonefish.

The bonefish is now too far away from me to see — fifty yards or more — and it races away with undiminished strength and speed. The fly rod is bent into a full arc as I lean back against the fish, and the steady shriek from from the fly reel has lost none of its high pitch. The line now seems to go straight out from the tip of the rod, parallel to the surface and stretching away toward the shimmering mangroves on the horizon; I can no longer see for certain where it actually enters the water, far out toward the center of the wide lagoon.

The tension goes out of the line. And then it goes slack.

Frantically I reel in, awkwardly trying to direct the re-spooling line evenly onto the arbor so it won't bunch up toward the end. There is still some slight resistance on the line as I reel, telling me that the fish is still on but swimming toward me; we're both pulling against the same arced belly of line out there in the lagoon. What I want is to get the slack out and put pressure again on the fish before it rests long enough to —

Take off again. Down goes the rod tip. Up comes the belly of line. Away goes the bonefish. Out goes the line I've been reclaiming.

This run is half as far as the first one, and not as strong. In a few seconds, there is enough weakness so that I can lean back and then give way, slowly pumping against the tension and reeling in line each time as I do. This lasts for an amount of time that I can't really measure even as I'm doing it, the bonefish coming toward me perhaps a foot or two with each bend, pull and reel. Several more times the process is broken as the bonefish turns and runs, taking line again, but these are short, pugnacious little battles, like you'd get at the beginning of a largemouth bass fight.

Now I can see the bonefish, twenty or thirty yards out as it tries to swim from the pressure, slanting away at right angles to me, finning steadily. It seems disappointingly small; from the initial run I'd thought it might be a six-pounder or better.

Finally I have the bonefish, and it's not until it swims quietly a rod's length away that I can see that it really is a good fish after all: twenty inches long, maybe more. Everything about a bonefish in the water is deceptive; even when you get a good look at one it keeps changing size. Reaching down, I lift the fish just enough to get at where it's been hooked. The bonefish is docile now, bright and muscular in my hands, skin iridescent as mother of pearl, its blinkless eye a circle of hammered gold around a tiny infinity of absolute black as it stares at, through and past me.

The fly comes out easily, a nice touch that isn't always the case with a species that sucks in its food like an underwater shop-vac, and I let the fish slide out of my hands. It rests upright in the calf-deep water, coasting slowly away and then gradually accelerating with no visible movement of any of its fins, a testament to the frictionless efficiency with which it moves through the water. I believe that if any of us ever carved an exact bonefish shape, rendered it neutrally buoyant and was able to cover it with a perfect artificial bonefish skin coating, then placed the carving in salt water, the inanimate sculpture would slide forward through the water on its own, gliding without restraint and propelled by a hydrodynamic principle as yet undiscovered by science.

The bonefish swims quietly away, finally disappearing under the surface sheen at the edge of where my polaroids can cut through it. Absently I run my fingers over the Lime Candy fly, smoothing back its chartreuse-died streaming hair and then sliding my fingertips up the leader tippet, feeling for abrasions. There aren't any, so I leave it alone.

I used to feel guilty about that, not changing the tippet after each fish, something the experts have always insisted on with the mechanically-accurate discipline that drives most of them, but I never could make myself do it unless I felt a bona fide, line-ruining nick on it. And I certainly don't want to change the fly, now that it's got some

genuine fish slime on it to make it smell more interesting to the next bonefish. I'll never carry one of those plastic bottles of bait scent with me, but when the real thing presents itself, I'll use it.

I'll use it later, however. Now I'm in no hurry to start stalking again. The best part of a good fish early in the day is the freedom to relax that it gives you. Even if you don't see another bonefish, the day itself has become a trophy, one to be counted against all the other days of this or any other year. How often really, do you even see a bonefish, let alone cast to one?

Let alone hold one in your hands.

So don't rush away from it. Sit down and have a cup of cold water from the green daypack. Settle your butt onto the warm sand above the tide line, let the sun hit the back of your shirt while you wait for something to happen, either out there, in the lagoon of clarity, or right here, in your own mind.

•   •   •

The qualities of a good bonefish flat are so universal and specific that any one of them could be lifted whole, carried away and transplanted on the edge of another island or atoll in any other ocean on the other side of the world. If you then went there for the first time, you'd have no idea that this transcendental grafting had happened at all: it would just be a good flat, as you expected it would be before you got there.

Biologists and the geologically-attuned will dispute this notion, of course. How, they'll want to know, can you not see the difference between the worn coral tops of a Guanaja barrier flat and the limestone strata of the Exuma uplift? And do you really think you'll find an Atlantic Gray Cowrie in Kiribati?

My answer is the same as the bonefish's: Say what? Strata who? Leave me alone. Where's dinner?

This universality is most apparent in the tackle catalogs, where the graphic designers go out of their way to pick photographs that could apply to any flat anywhere while somewhere on the same page they try to sell you separate and expensive subsets of the limited

number of bonefish and permit flies they offer: the Christmas Island Collection, the Belize Selection, Pete's Permit Permutation, Baedecker's Bonefish Biters. And so on. Better make that "bitters" for old Baedecker, to go with the gin-clear water in the catalog photo.

But do take a closer look at that photo, the one with the guide crouched and pointing off the page while the angler in bright new tropical wear launches a loop-perfect cast as he stares through his optically-correct fishing glasses toward a fish that you and I know is not even there. Of course we know they're not really fishing, but can you tell me what flat they're posing on? All you ever see in the distance is flat oceanic horizon or a thin smudge of mangrove. I couldn't say which hemisphere they're in.

The fishing magazines are more informative in this regard, as the article accompanying the pictures is usually about a specific place and often about a specific trip there. But professional fishing writers are seldom victims of "you shoulda been here yesterday." They, of course, are the guys who *were* there yesterday, even if they actually were still on the plane from New York. Or further back than that. The article their editors want to publish won't usually have the word "skunk" in it, so the writers do what the rest of us do after they get back home. They lie. It's a time-honored fishing tradition that the magazines take a step further by slipping in a few pictures that might not have been taken on the same trip their correspondent is now chronicling. They might not, for that matter, have been taken

on the same flats. Or even in the same hemisphere.

I find this all to be very disconcerting. Without a sense of place to center me, I don't really want to go fishing in the first place. Even in the middle of a cast to a single bonefish that's about to detect that I'm there, with all the game riding on this one presentation and locked into a cone of concentration as I try to connect with this one shadow moving toward me, I have to know exactly where I am. And how I got there.

I have to know where I am not just geographically — although this is a base requirement that must come first — but I want also to feel all the other human connections that can moor each of us to a place, binding us to it forever even before we've sensed that it's happening. Building these links, the ones that hold even when we're no longer there, takes time and it takes that time away from the fishing itself, something you won't want to allow.

But if you travel enough to one place, as I have the Bahamas, and even if you travel there only to go fishing, this time away will present itself to you whether you want it or not, on its own terms and unbidden. Rain will fall, wind will rise, a minor ailment will afflict you, or perhaps you'll just have to take a day or an afternoon off. That's the time, and it's a gift. Take it.

What I like to do, here in the Bahamas, is to walk inland, following a sandy island road away from the docks and the harbor and out through town. If you feel like being alone, listening to not much more than your own thoughts and a bit of tropical wind moving through the kind of plants you don't see at home, then go out in the hot early afternoon, when most of the residents will be under some shade.

Almost immediately you'll forget why you started this walk. Here on the outskirts of town, there will be houses still close together, built of cinder blocks covered with smoothed stucco and painted bright whites and soft pinks, light green or

sometimes not painted at all. Their windows will be open rectangles into dark interiors whose coolness you can feel even from out here on the sun-baked road. In small fenced yards of hard ground, spare grasses and broken limestone, there will be a chicken or two, perhaps a dog, a sleeping cat that never comes indoors. From a radio inside one of the houses an announcer from Nassau will be reciting a listing of upcoming church services, noting a change in the mail boat schedule or reading obituaries recently received from the outer islands.

As you travel farther from town, your attention will swing from houses to the land itself, rising only slightly from sea level and crowded with wild vegetation, lower, harder, scrubbier and drier than you might have expected, here on what you thought was a tropical island. No point in all the Bahamas rises above 400 feet and most of the islands, like this one, are much lower. There are no rivers, no flowing springs, no water table to sustain the sort of year-round lushness that over time cycles itself into the jungles found on other islands in similar latitudes. Here the daily showers and drenching storms drop water that drains quickly through the porous ground while the toughened root systems of bull vine, bromeliad and casuarinas soak up a daily ration.

But it's a generous enough portion. Here on the walk from town, you'll see wild tamarind and pigeon plum trees, oleander and escaped mangoes, yucca plants, cactuses and wild coffee, hibiscus and poinciana, all in a muted, sun-bleached spectrum that's nonetheless full-range, as if the floral colors and green foliation, after so many generations of salt wash and sun strike, have naturally selected toward their habitat, reflecting the low, exposed profile of the islands themselves.

This trick of the light, this excessive brightness that even a good pair of sunglasses can't restore to the full contrast your mind wants and expects, will of course be accentuated here in the midafternoon, with the sun not far enough past

apogee to have dipped perceptibly, with every shadow still beaten back and shriveled almost invisible under the plant that later, as the sun falls, will throw it longer, darker and bolder.

Occasionally, as the road circles a bit higher and further from town, you'll begin to get glimpses of the water, stretching deep and blue out from the ocean side of the island and mottling paler and sand-washed on the shallow side, where the flats are. Where you were yesterday, and where you'll be again tomorrow.

At about this point on the walk, I like to find an elevated, wind-washed vantage and sit down, taking in the distant flats and wandering blue channels, the deepwater horizon, studying them in detail until I begin to lose my concentration, staring and progressively losing focus until finally, in a sun-flicker of island clarity, I see myself, out there on the flats, staring back.

· · ·

I awake with a start. Here on the sand spit in my lagoon, I'm still sitting down after the first bonefish of the day, and I've dozed off, just enough to need an internal reset. Who am I? Where am I? What time is it? Hal Borland's questions, here in the Bahamas. Did he ever go bonefishing? I don't think so. Maybe.

Once again on my feet, I look around. Mid morning now and nothing has changed. The wind is still absent, the salt surface glassy, no one else here. It is getting hotter. I pick up the lighter of the

two rods, with the Lime Candy fly hooked in the keeper, and walk back into the water.

This time I prepare myself better. Wading out to knee-deep water I pull line from the reel and false cast, gently driving the lingering stiffness from my right arm and getting a proper length of fly line out and ready. I pick up the fly and hold it by the bend of the hook in my right hand while I loosely grasp two loops with my left; if the wading gets deeper I'll shift the loops to my mouth, but for now this hand holding will do.

I decide to circle the lagoon slowly, moving counter clockwise in order to keep the sun mostly to my back. The channel through which all the filling new tidal water now runs is in the other direction, off toward the right, and I know that any newly-arriving fish will come in that way. But I don't want to try to ambush them as they enter, something that in other, earlier times I would have done. In other, earlier times I wouldn't have dozed off, either.

But I've learned. And one thing I've learned the hard way is that traveling bonefish don't come to the fly as readily as those that have made it all the way to their feeding areas. So what I want is to be up in those feeding areas, waiting for them as they slide in with the tide. All I have to do now is find a good place, one that looks good to me and to the bonefish, and then I have to be patient and stay alert.

Should be easy, I decide, moving easily on the hard bottom here in the still-sandy section where the first fish struck. Fifty yards ahead of me the water is darker with turtle grass and other bottom life that I've never learned to name; if there are fish there, they will be much harder to see. A problem I'll tune into when I get to it.

Something splashes out in the middle of the lagoon, more of a showering hiss than a loud plunk, and I turn quickly to see. All that remains is a rippling patch of disturbed surface, about the size of a throw rug, a dark mottling of the surface sheen a hundred yards away. Intently I watch, hoping to see the telltale bulges of displaced water that will signal the underwater direction of travel of whatever caused the commotion. The water calms itself; no wake shows me the way. Nothing.

Nothing. The lagoon is quiet again, dissolving its secrets as I watch, shielding them with mirages, reflections and a liquification of the very light that wants to illuminate them for me. I immediately want to head toward where the disturbance was, instinctively wanting to move toward something on which I can focus, toward this point of demonstrated presence even as it disappears from actual sight. But it's a reaction easily contained; whatever caused the splash will have moved by the time I get there. That spot will, in fact, be the one part of the entire lagoon where that particular fish — or school of fish — will not be. Or, more accurately, will least likely be. Statistical analysis gets at very faint probabilities by calculating the odds of that thing not happening,

and this makes sense to me on a bonefish flat, where only the sea cucumbers seem to stay put.

So I continue on my steady way toward the back of the lagoon, a third of a mile away. There are mangroves back there, low, thin and spread out; colonizing young mangroves with knee-high, arching roots, the kind that you can with some care walk through without crouching and contorting and threatening to break your equipment. This is good to see, for bonefish will feed up into and among them as the tide fills the edges of the lagoon, flooding the glistening wet sand on which the mangroves now stand.

The bottom under my feet changes as I walk, hunting. My eyes are on the water at the limit of polaroid penetration — maybe fifty or seventy-five yards away — so the change is something I feel before I see it. I look down. I'm in the turtle grass.

I don't know why it's called this: turtle grass. It isn't grass and I've never seen a turtle anywhere near it. But then again it looks like grass, albeit wider, heavier and with a rasp to it that no suburban lawnkeeper would tolerate. And it is only ankle high, short for any lawn I ever had responsibility for; there haven't been many, and most of them, come to think of it, did look a lot like this stuff I'm now walking through. And perhaps turtles do eat it, a detail of Caribbean biodiversity that I ought to have learned by now. I'll try to remember to ask Roland when he comes back with the skiff late this afternoon. What time is it, anyway?

I look at my watch, a concession I concede to the ticking increments only out of respect for Roland's workday. He doesn't want to stay out here on the flats past his supper time any more than I want to ask him to do it, although I'm sure he would if I did.

Splash! Ten feet in front of me. A gray shape streamlines away in a dodging blur, leaving behind a boil that says " . . . and a good one, too."

The bonefish doesn't even slow down until it's out of sight.

Well, damn again. I do this every day at least once. Step on one. Usually it's the point bone for a school of a dozen or more, causing an eruption in front of me like a load of pea gravel flung hard at the water.

This time it's only one, an even sadder tale that tells me it was probably bigger than it looked.

My concentration is now renewed. Half the morning is gone, but the rest of the day lies ahead and I know there will be fish in it. Meanwhile I think I'll get away from this turtle grass — it's more sensitive than it looks and no one should stomp through it if there's a good way to avoid it. I'll slide a bit to the left, closer to the beach where I'm less likely to spook one.

•   •   •

When you work the flats from a boat you don't usually have lapses of concentration that affect specific fish. Because you have to take turns in the casting position, you naturally stay alert while you're up there, reserving your time in the middle seat for doping off and tuning out. But I usually have trouble not doing that, dozing while sitting, and I often do miss seeing things then that I wouldn't have had I been better keyed in to the action at hand, like I am when I'm on my feet up in the bow of the boat.

One time nodding off in a skiff I missed seeing something I had been expectantly looking for for years, ever since Roland's cousin Albert had told me about it: the feeding rush of dolphins up in the shallows. Albert had smiled just at the thought of it.

"They throw wahtah, mon. Some high up." He had lifted both hands to demonstrate, almost dropping his pole in the process. "Whoosh!" He grinned.

Whoosh, for certain. I had no trouble envisaging it: dashing gray bodies half out of the water, dorsals high, sprinting and swirling, accelerating fast enough to catch fleeing bonefish, throwing sheets of water ten or twelve feet in the air. God's own jet ski, but with an honest purpose and the access rights of a true native. I couldn't wait to witness it.

When they did appear those years later, three or four of them working together, Becky and Roland thought — "Look at that!" she had exclaimed — I had to snap awake and look around.

I turned first the wrong way and then the correct, but all I caught up to was the flailed water and fast-disappearing wakes of the instant action. A hundred yards of flat behind the gone dolphins was churned to a frothing brown. Nesting birds had lifted from the mangroves, shrieking and circling upward. Foot-high waves were coming our way from where it had all happened.

"Did you see that?" Becky breathed.

"Unbelievable," was what I said, in what might have been the single most appropriately generic remark I have ever uttered. I think she still believes I was describing the dolphins and not myself.

There are no dolphins today, here in the lagoon. Maybe ever in the lagoon; it's much too shallow for them, I'm certain, unless —

There are tailing bonefish. A hundred yards from me, up toward the head of the lagoon, near the scattered mangroves. More than one. How could I have missed them before? Have they just appeared?

Well, it doesn't matter, does it? Just look at them. Calmly feeding, totally unaware, just over there. The tails coming up one or two at a time as the fish tip and root among the bottom sands; three or four inches of upright caudal fin switching to and fro, catching the sunlight in a fluid waver of translucent silver brushed with gold.

A bonefish tail, gently waggling above a quiet surface, is like an antler gleam in the morning, quietly slipping through the November gray of a northern woodlot. So often and and for so long have you envisaged it that the actual, shining presence of the thing here in front of you tends

perversely to carry you farther from, rather than closer to, the physical reality it now so plainly presents. It's like those trick video shots where the camera rushes toward something while the cameraman runs the zoom in reverse, expanding the field of view; you seem to rush toward and away from it at the same time.

But I won't rush here, either toward or away from the tailing bonefish. They're still far enough away so I can drop the Lime Candy fly, roll some line forward and shoot out a good start on the fifty feet or more I'll want when I make the real cast. Carefully bringing the line back in and gathering it in two big loops trailing from my left hand, I leave the started line hanging from the tip top of the rod as I run my fingers down the leader to pick the fly up once again. Now I'm ready to stalk them.

They're still feeding, still unconcerned. Tails come regularly out of the water now; it can't be more than a foot deep where they are, about the same as here. This is pretty sweet, with the wind

down and out. I've never mastered the sort of overhead, wrist-tilting thing you're supposed to do to make a right-handed cast that lets the line go past your left shoulder with a stiff wind on your starboard beam. I haven't whacked my eye yet, but the back of my neck got punctured more than once before I gave up trying it in favor of a roundabout

stalk to get the wind over my left shoulder or at least somewhere behind me.

Not here, though. The flat is glassy and the wind gone elsewhere. How far away is the wind? I wonder as I move toward the wobbling tails. Hispaniola, randomly, comes into my mind. I wonder who was the first European to see a New World bonefish. Probably some shipwrecked unfortunate, delirious and chasing shadows in the shimmering heat of the thirsty flats . . .

The bonefish ahead of me are no longer stationary. Still feeding, but they're definitely on the move. Angling more to my right, I recalculate a route to intercept them, forcing myself to go slowly. To go quietly. They definitely are moving, and it's not in this direction.

There is a thumb rule here: If you can hear the swoosh of water as you drag your legs through the water, then you're going too fast. The problem is that almost any speed at all makes that swoosh; if the bonefish ahead of you are on the go, then either you keep quiet and never catch them, or you go fast enough to keep up and the resultant disturbance causes the skitterish fish to move just a bit further away, just a bit quicker. So you pick up the pace, sloshing even louder . . .

With all the gear the catalog companies keep adding to the flats fisherman's required list, I'm confused as to why they haven't addressed this need. Hydrodynamic design has long since solved the problem: Have you ever noticed the wake behind any of Dennis Conner's sailboats? No? That's because there isn't any. The water closes behind his fleeing fantail like congressional mouths after a big-money fundraiser: fast, tight and without making any waves. I know there is no impediment to adapting this technology to the flats wader; I see a pair of tapered extensions attached to the ankles of your wading booties, light as snakeproof leggings, reaching about knee-high and streamlined like a racing sloop's keel so you can just about sprint through the water leaving not even a bubble . . .

The bonefish have settled down again, feeding in one spot. Only seventy yards or so now. I slow down, sliding carefully through the water that doesn't quite reach my knees. This is getting sweeter by the minute.

When they're about a hundred feet away, I try to get a good look at them, craning upward and tilting my head from side to side to optimize the polarizing effect of my glasses. There seem to be a half dozen bonefish, milling calmly about, with two or three at any moment with their tails up, feeding; I'm close enough to hear the slight slurping sound of their waggling caudals. It's becoming harder to stay calm.

As I very slowly creep forward, crouching slightly, I let go of the fly and roll cast some fly line out on the water, at an angle away from the fish. Not wanting to take my eyes off the bonefish, I nonetheless know that I have to; I have to make sure there aren't any others close enough to me to be spooked by the false casts I'm about to make.

Furtive as a shoplifter I glance to my right and left: I see no other bonefish. The ones in front of me are now seventy or eighty feet away, calm as a road crew on lunch break. I lift a backcast against the line laying out on the water in front of me; the Lime Candy fly makes a tiny ploop as it breaks the surface tension.

The bonefish erupt in a splashy panic, scattering wildly before my backcast has even straightened. I let the cast dissipate behind me, wilting and dropping onto the water as the fish disappear, pushing bow waves out toward the center of the lagoon, leaving behind them a milky patch of water near the shoreline, billowing with upchurned marl and sand.

I don't even move. The fly rod still points backward, toward all the slack line behind me. Slowly the wakes from the fled fish dispel against the mangrove shoots and the sloping beach. I watch for a long time as the water re-clarifies itself, until there is no longer any sign that the bonefish were here.

The sun is hot on my back and a brine of perspiration has formed just above my upper lip. Once again the lagoon is quieter than church, except for a faint, distant ringing in my ears. Taking a long breath, I look up and away and take off my hat. Far out to the west, a cotton fluff of small cumulus has appeared, the first cloud of the day, rising, calling for a distant wind.

•　•　•

What is it that makes a fish a sport fish? A baseline requirement, of course, is that it wants to eat something that can be attached to a hook. Vegetarians and plankton-eaters like mullet and whale sharks are out, then, although I suppose either one would be interesting on a fly rod. Among the hookables, if a species is predatory — preferring, say, live ballyhoo to pressed doughballs — then it will line up higher on the sporting scale by virtue of its requisite aggressiveness and speed in the water. Near the top of this gamut will be the select, hard-to-catch few with the schizoid personalities of street muggers: opportunistic, hungry, remorseless and scared of their own shadows. Striped bass in the daylight, brown trout in clear streams. Bonefish up on the flats, as I've just had re-demonstrated. I don't even want to talk about permit.

Except that, here in the lagoon of recently unwanted clarity, I keep seeing one. Or at least I think I do.

It started almost as soon as I got out of Roland's skiff, now several hours ago. Far across the lagoon a glint of reflected light, thin and upright in the water, caught my eye. It seemed to move, darkening as it changed its angle against the light, looking in the distance like a bent feather sticking up and out of the water, and then it was gone.

I knew it was a permit even as I told myself it probably wasn't. Wishing up a permit on a flat where there might actually be one is a distraction that will blossom toward dementia if you let it have its head, especially out here alone, with only the mad dogs and Englishmen for company. The vision was just that, I told myself, and I put it away. Until now.

Because it's back again. Out in the middle of the lagoon this time, maybe two hundred yards away, a flexing sickle shape waving gently a few inches above the undisturbed surface. A foot behind it, parallel, arcing the same way, a matching dark feather comes out, flicks against the water, and they both vanish as one.

That's a permit. That's a feeding permit. And I can walk to it. A rush that starts as an indistinct thump behind my heart spreads up and into my head, pressing an almost electric pulsing through my sinuses; I can feel my ears burn.

It's definitely time to change the Lime Candy fly. Keeping my eyes on the center of the lagoon, I start walking quickly that way, not even trying to be quiet. I tuck the fly rod under my arm as I run my finger down the leader until I have the fly in hand. My clippers are on a loop of monofilament around my neck; I don't have to look down in order to detach the fly and slip it into a shirt pocket. I reach into the other pocket and lift out the little blue plastic change-purse in which I keep my permit flies.

I had one of these change-purses as a kid and had thought them to be as irretrievably gone as the Fifties themselves until I spotted one in a convenience store a couple of years ago. You might recognize it: a two-inch flattened oval of soft plastic with a slit running lengthwise so that it pops open like a mouth when you squeeze the ends, something you can do in the palm of one hand. It holds three

or four flies nicely, in this case all crab imitations, two small ones of hair and feathers and a couple of larger epoxy flies. With the clipped leader in my mouth, I finger among the permit crabs and lift out the larger of the hair-and-feather versions. No science here; I just like to cast weightless flies.

I do have to stop to tie on the crab, and I take some care doing it: This is a permit. I even remember to dip the fly into the water and squeeze it, driving out any infinitesimal bubbles that might keep it from sinking on the first cast. Ready now, I step off again toward where the permit had been. But where exactly was that?

There is no sign of the fish, and it gives me pause. Remembering my earlier admonition that the one place that it will not be is where it was, I stop. If the permit has moved, which it certainly has, then it might have swum in my direction. It could be somewhere near me right now. Stepping on a bonefish is one thing; spooking a permit would be grounds for . . .

Settle down. Slow down. Take a breath and scan carefully. And no more swooshing through the water. This is a permit.

Twenty minutes later I've seen nothing. Moving cautiously and scanning in all directions, I've been out to where the permit was — or where I think it was — and then I've waded carefully in the direction those two sickle fins had indicated the permit might be moving. Nowhere has the water been much more than knee deep, but that's two feet. A big permit can hide in less, and I don't think this was a large one.

A large one? Until now I hadn't even considered how big or small it was. Wondering about the size of a permit is like worrying over how many millions there are in this week's Lotto drawing. Exactly, in fact, like that.

The permit is gone. As if it had never been here. Did I really see it? Well, yes. Of course I did.

Really? Yes. Twice. You don't believe me? Whatever you say.

In outward quiet I stand here, in the middle of the lagoon. Enough of these quibbling little debates. I'm here to silence them, remember? And the remaining point is this, unequivocal:

There is a permit here now, swimming either in the shallow water of this lagoon or in the depths of my imagination, and for the rest of the day I will have to hunt for it. If not in one place, then in the other.

• • •

From out here in the center of the lagoon, I have a better view of the channel through which Roland ran me in here. It's deeper than I remembered, or than it seemed from the boat anyway. Where it cuts through the mangroves from outside, the water is well over my head — a flowing, indistinct palette of darker greens and intermittent blues that describe the tide-scoured bottom of the channel — and it stays deep for a much greater distance into the lagoon than I had known. Or expected; it's going to be tricky, I now see, to get across it to fish the other side of the lagoon.

I could swim it, of course, but that's a hard thing to do while keeping the fly reel out of the salt water. Plus I'd then be on the other side of the channel from my daypack, still sitting on the sand spit where I left it. Out here you don't want to place too many barriers between yourself and something to drink. Or something to eat. Almost instantly I'm hungry, a pathetically transparent physical reaction to a mental stimulus that even

Pavlov would reject as being nothing more than a conditioning to conditioning itself.

Well, speak for yourself, Ivan: You never had a conch fritter sandwich on local bread. I turn toward the sand spit just as something flashes, deep in the channel. I stop.

A jack, probably. A blue runner or a bar jack, maybe. They'll surely be down in a flowing cafeteria like this one, now running with the flooding tide, steady as an upland stream.

Jacks are a great sportfish, high on the chain of artificial lure chasers, but giving away some degree-of-difficulty points in the process. Like a bluefish, they'll hit anything. I hardly ever pass up a chance to cast to either one.

But here I've got a problem. The jacks will be down deeper than I can reach with my floating fly line. The choice is to put on some sort of baitfish-imitating streamer — the crab might work, but I don't want to lose it on a jack — and try to entice one up by fast-stripping the streamer a few inches under the surface; or I can try a popper.

I'll try the popper first, a small, foam-bodied skipping bug that works well on striped bass at home. It usually doesn't work here, though, but the strike is so vicious when it does that I always put it on first. And then end up keeping it on too long, hoping cast after cast that this next try will be the one.

Casting the wind-resistant bug is awkward, but subtlety is no requirement here. I flop the popper down on the far side of the inflowing channel, about forty feet away, and immediately begin a staccato series of short yanks as it arcs downcurrent and across, jerking and splashing its way back to my side.

I see the fish coming before it strikes, almost in slow motion, an accelerating dark streak in the center of the channel that flashes bright silver at the surface as it turns and splashes, grabbing the popper, and I strike instinctively as soon as I feel it. Immediately the following things happen, overlapping and instantaneous:

The line loses its resistance and the popper comes back toward me. The fish vanishes back down into the green water.

And I realize it wasn't slow motion. It was a baby tarpon.

I've never caught a tarpon in the Bahamas. Before this little one, I'd only seen three in all the islands and they were together, cruising on the outside of a reef on the south side of Grand Bahama as Becky and I and Leroy flashed by on a high speed plane, running from one flat to another in the middle of a bright afternoon. But even at that speed Leroy had spotted them, immediately cutting the throttle and spinning the skiff back toward the long, dark shapes he had seen against the bright sand bottom forty feet below. We all saw them then, a trio of four-foot-long tarpon that waited until we were about to idle right over them before flicking their tails and sliding away toward deeper water. None of us had even reached for a rod.

Tarpon that size are really rare in the Bahamas, and as far as I know they never appear on the flats. But there are some cays that have these three- to six-pounders in fishable numbers; on Long Island, I've heard, you can with some probability expect to get them, especially if you go up into the mangroves near Deadman's Cay.

Not here, though. Not on this island, as far as anyone has told me, and certainly not in this lagoon.

But on the other hand, I tell myself, peering closely into the shifting aquamarine of the channel as I strip in line for another cast, I'm not going to tell anyone about this. Even, I say . . . lifting my backcast . . . if for some unbelievably lucky chance . . . the line straightens behind me . . . there just happens . . . I lean with my shoulder into the forward throw . . . to maybe be . . . the line shoots and the popper hits the water . . . against all odds . . . I begin the skipping retrieve . . . one more . . .

Tarpon. Just like the other one, shooting up from below, flashing silver, taking the bug, turning and heading back down. One . . . two . . .

Three. Hit him. Hard! Hit him again. Very hard!

The tarpon is in the air, four body lengths of shaking, water-thrashing impulses that sound in the still lagoon like wet wings flapping, before ker-plunking back down with a sudden hard pull on the line, ripping the slack from my left hand and snapping it taught against the reel, and the fish back in the air, water flying, tarpon wild shaking and then the fish runs upstream, sprinting for the open water ouside the lagoon. I have no idea how to set the drag for this, so I just try to hold the rod tip up and lean against the running fish which suddenly turns back and goes airborne again, fifty yards away. This tarpon is no six pounds. Easily twice that. Back in the water the fish turns and bolts for the mangrove channel.

I won't have enough backing for this. My fly reel is screeching non-stop at a pitch I haven't heard from it before. With no choice, I tighten the drag.

Now it seems the rod will be pulled from my grip. I plant the butt cap against my hip bone and lean back against the fish and hang on, stressing the whole rig as the tarpon steadily drains the backing.

I once tied a ten-pound bag of dog food to a fly rod set up with a twelve-pound tippet and then tried to pick the bag up off the floor, holding the rod the way I am right now here in the lagoon, as if fighting a fish. I chickened out long before the kibble left the floor because I couldn't make myself believe the rod wasn't about to break, the tension was so extreme. But it turned out to be no failed experiment: I've leaned harder into all the fish I've fought after that, happily shortening every post-hookup encounter that has occurred since.

Shortening a fish fight is a good thing on almost every level, good for you and better for the fish, as long as you don't take it to the unforgivable extreme of the tournament bassmasters who simply jerk them into the boat as soon as they're hooked, a

grotesque motion whose sporting counterpart can best be seen around the greed rail of a casino craps table.

Well, nobody ever jerked a hooked tarpon quickly anywhere, although the big fish/light tackle experts have for some time now espoused the side-to-side method whereby you hold the rod parallel to the water and pull at an acute angle aganst the direction the fish wants to go; as soon as the fish responds by turning, you flop the rod over hard the other way and do a reciprocal pull against this new direction. It sounds effective, probably works as advertised, and I can't make myself do it.

Not that I get attached very often to record-potential fish, but even against a small tarpon like this one, where I'm sure the side-pressure method would tire the fish much quicker, I still have to keep the fly rod high and upright, arcing classically in a tradition that comfortably predates the IGFA. There aren't very many venues in life in which you can truly visualize yourself in action, but fighting a good fish is one of them. I don't know about you, but I don't want to see myself all bent over, doing something sideways so I can get it over with sooner.

Finally, the fish turns. I begin to crank some line back onto the reel. And although there will be another several runs and a few more jumps, this is now a settled fish fight, unless something comes up snake eyes, like the hook pulling out, a possibility that remains. Like all my terminal stuff, the popper out there in the tarpon's mouth has its barb pinched down.

But it stays put, and eventually — I couldn't tell you how long. Ten minutes? Forty? No, not that

much — the tarpon is in front of me, staying upright and finning weakly at the edge of the channel. Grasping the leader and tucking the rod under one arm, I take the pliers out of my shirt pocket and reach in to pull out the hook which is stuck just inside the tarpon's mouth. It comes out with an easy curl of my wrist at the same moment that the tarpon flicks away from me and begins steadily to swim back down into the current, sinking from sight, blending and darkening, disappearing finally against the bottle green variations of the channel's shifting bottom. For a long time I look down there, my mind emptied of ordered thoughts. I never even touched the fish.

•   •   •

Tarpon thrive in the warm Atlantic and Caribbean wherever flowing fresh water empties into an area of shallow reefs and tidal flats; you can fish for them at the mouths of tropical rivers from Central America to the west coast of Africa. And even though the greatest concentration of them anywhere in the world is in and around the Florida Keys, washed by the River of Grass itself, the best guess of the biologists is that there never will be many at all here in the Bahamas, just a hundred or two miles away. Not, at least, until some fresh water starts flowing in some quantity from one or two of these islands. Why there are any at all is something of a mystery, but then again so is a lot of tarpon natural history.

I do hope the biologists are right. Envisioning the tranquil flats of the Bahamas inhabited by large tarpon is one of my recurring nightmares. There is a quiet balance to these waters now, a one-rod-will-do-it-all sort of symmetry that, for me, is near the heart of why I fish here, an attraction that not many seem to share with me. And that, of course, preambles the nightmare: an invasion of celebrity Keys guides and their interchangeable Type-A clientele waving twelve-weight technology all over places like this quiet lagoon.

Well, it won't happen, at least not soon and certainly never on anything like an Islamorada-in-May scale. For now I think I will wade back over to my sandy little spit of dry ground, settle down on the soft beach and eat the conch sandwich I brought with me. I might even celebrate that magic little tarpon with the Kalik beer I brought along for the ride home, maybe opening the bottle right now with the same pliers I used to release the fish.

In fact, I say to myself as I start back, I know I will.

• • •

*I*t's about noon now, I think as I sit on the sand spit in the unbroken sunlight of my day alone in the lagoon. Close enough, anyway, that I don't feel any need to check the estimate against my watch. A few afternoon clouds are beginning to gather in the four distances from here, out over the ocean and farther inland, across the interior heat of the island. But their effect, if it comes at all, is still hours away.

Finishing my conch sandwich and the beer I promoted to midday consumption, I've decided to fish for the first part of the afternoon with my heavier eight-weight rod overloaded with a nine-weight line. The permit is still out there somewhere, and I do want to try to find a big barracuda. The odds of tarpon reappearing are low, but it all adds up to a good argument for heavier tackle to throw bigger flies. So I'm sitting here getting ready to go, checking the Pliobond-coated knot that attaches the fly line to the leader butt. I like this knot; I once went fishing with the man who invented it.

Jimmy Albright drifted down from Detroit to the Florida Keys in 1935, looking for something to do for a few weeks, and he stayed. He was still there on a rain-washed day in the spring of 1990 when a friend and I showed up for the day at Bud n' Mary's, an Islamorada boat dock that had been there almost as long as he had. Jimmy was there ahead of us, waiting in his skiff.

I'd seen him the day before, staked out in a pass, waiting for tarpon as we went by in another flats boat, heading for our own pass. He had a couple of older sports in the boat then, and the three of them were sitting down, drifting live mullet, waiting for a hit.

"Jimmie's asleep," said Joe, our guide.

And I guess he was. Facing aft with his arms folded across the poling platform and his head resting on his arms. As we passed by, there was a splashing out behind their boat, down-tide and about where their bait should have been. The mullet was thrashing circles around its cork, and then the water burst. A three-foot barracuda came straight up, two body lengths out of the water, twisting in the hazy sunlight, and in one headshake

at the top of the jump threw the mullet ten more feet into the air. Both of the fish came back down onto the surface, throwing white water halfway back to the boat.

Jimmie slowly lifted his head, turned back to the two sports who had just gotten their rods out of the holders and said something.

"Didn't seem too excited about it, did they?" I said.

"He's seen it before," said Joe.

"What?" I asked. "The 'cuda or his clients asleep at the switch?"

Joe just smiled.

The next morning it was windy and raining, and the marine forecast could have been summed up in a single four-letter word. Bob and I went down to the dock anyway, and there was Jimmie, waiting.

"Fly fishing's out," he said. "I bought some mullet from the girl."

By most accounts, the first time anyone

intentionally fly fished for bonefish was when Joe Brooks tried it with streamers in 1947. Jimmie Albright was his guide that day. They caught fish.

You don't get many chances to hook so directly into the grand history of something, and I didn't want to miss my chance with the man who showed Joe Brooks how. Mullet or bucktail, polaroids or rain gear, we were definitely on for the ride.

The ride turned out to be a long, wide tour of the Keys backcountry, reefs and flats sliding by in the varying gray of the day's stationary front. We stopped twice and staked out, soaking bait and seeing an occasional rolling tarpon. We hooked our own barracuda, and no one was asleep.

And in between, we talked with Jimmie. Lying easy over a tide-flooded flat, Bob or I would ask if this was a good spot for bonefish. Jimmie would scan across the flat.

"Yeah," he'd answer, and he'd look long and hard at the water. Long and hard. "Pretty good."

A little coarse arithmetic says that, at that point, Jimmie had had something north of 10,000 days on this water, guiding guys who wanted to know if it was good for bonefish. Or tarpon. Or permit.

Yeah. Pretty good.

Toward the end of the day, we took a very long ride to a place where the bridges were down against the horizon, and the nearest keys were smudges in the afternoon gloom. Faintly dark in the water underneath us appeared a reef. We stopped and put out the bait, letting it swim down-tide. For a long time none of us spoke, and I turned back to see if Jimmie had nodded off. His arms were folded on the poling platform, but he wasn't asleep.

"First time I saw this place," Jimmie said, "there were five thousand tarpon rolling here." He paused, looked around. "Course that was almost fifty years ago."

A little while later we picked up the bait and headed in.

I've always used an Albright knot to connect a leader butt to a fly line, even before that day and especially since, and maybe you should, too. It'll be a bit bulkier than you might prefer, off-center, and it won't pass through the guides very smoothly. You'll want to coat it over with some sort of covering.

But unlike some of the newer, quicker, thinner versions, it absolutely will not unravel. No matter what's pulling on the other end. Or how long it pulls.

This one, the Albright I tied a couple of years ago, is still holding just fine. The leader is new from the mid section down, and I'm pretty much ready to go. But before I decide whether to attach a crab imitation for the permit or a counterfeit needlefish for a shot at a barracuda, I'm going to finish this conch sandwich, here in the Bahamian sunshine at the edge of the quiet lagoon, and let the relative merits of each weigh themselves in my mind.

•   •   •

Dan O'Brien in his beautiful book *Equinox* describes his friend Marshall Cutchin fighting a large permit in Belize, standing on the bow of the skiff and playing the fish with his eyes closed:

"I was whooping and hollering, shouting advice faster than the guide. The boat seemed frantic with activity until I realized that only the guide and I were frantic. Marshall was calm, eyes closed as if he were taking a beautiful woman into his arms. He was swaying and palmed the reel as gently as you would touch a sleeping child. He smiled as though he could hear cello music, but he kept the rod tip high. When the fish went left, he tilted the rod right. When the fish went right, he tilted left. When the fish allowed it, he reeled. When it wouldn't, he let it run. It took over twenty minutes to bring that permit to the boat and in all that time Marshall never opened his eyes, never uttered a word, never changed expression."

There aren't many of us with that kind of equanimity and fewer still who could convey it as brilliantly as does Dan O'Brien, parenthetically in a book centered around falconry in South Dakota. But *Equinox* is all about connections between us and living things less tamed, and Dan knew a real one when he saw it.

That passage from the book has been with me since I first read it, playing itself in my mind almost as often as I go fishing, and it's here again, with me in the lagoon. I'm holding the long, green needlefish fly in my hand and right now I want to know how Marshall Cutchin would react to a hooked barracuda, a really big and vicious one that attacked his fly from twenty yards away, struck with a turning ferocity that tried to yank the rod from his hands and then greyhounded, more out of the water than in, for an arrow-straight, surface-frothing hundred yards. I think you can get arrested for trying to hold that kind of woman in your arms, and you may lose body parts if you do it with your eyes closed.

Here in the lagoon my eyes are wide enough open, and what they're seeing is an unclear choice.

The only thing rarer than a permit on a fly rod is that same arced fly rod handled by a lone wader, but these are measurements taken from an angling universe already finely delineated. How many people, after all, have ever even been to a flat like this lagoon, have ever seen a free-swimming predator cruising in water half as deep as the fish is long? And how many of them have then cast to one, let alone done it with a fly rod while hunting with that predator fish in the same confined place?

What effete computation is it that says the permit is the better quarry here than a barracuda? Maybe we should all close our eyes more often when we fish. Or open them wider. Whichever.

Maybe.

My mind is settled. I tie on the permit fly.

Hey, what did you expect? This is fishing; you do what your heart says.

• • •

I've already decided that if I see any bonefish, I'm going to throw the permit fly at them unless they're so far away when I spot them that I have time to change. Prissy inventory management is something I left behind the last time I had a good job — you can decide cause and effect there for yourself — and I'm not about to reprise it here in the hard-won lagoon of island clarity. This decision grants me a temporarily settled mind as I set out once again toward the back of the lagoon, wading quietly and skirting around the turtle grass. The sun is very high, almost directly overhead, and everything in the water now stands out in a crisp, three-dimensional lucidity beneath the unriffled surface, itself completely invisible for fifty feet in every direction around me. I take off my polaroids and there is the surface sheen, a washed-out reflection of the pale blue sky; I put them back on and it vanishes, uncovering every grain of sand, every strand of weed, every tiny sea shell, presenting them in a perfectly clear but slightly wobbled distortion that is the only hint there is any water over them at all.

English wants another word to describe this, and I wonder for a minute if the Arawaks had a complex lexicon of water descriptors, like the Inuit people have for snow. But of course they didn't have polaroids, so they might be as lost as I am now to render it. It is, this tangible mirage that moves with me in places like this, as much as anything else here, why I keep coming back to the Bahamas, and why I walk the flats so much when I do.

Becky and I once went with some good fishing friends on a week-long trip with the specific purpose of bonefishing at night. Lynn Drayton dreamed it up after reading an article in, I think, *Florida Sportsman* magazine. The idea was that if you got a full moon, the combination of extreme tides and shadow-casting moonlight made it possible, even effective, to wander the flats at midnight, listening for tailing bones and throwing flies at them. It sounded suspiciously like an outdoor writer pouring Nantucket and Andros into a blender and discarding the striped bass, but we went along anyway, demonstrating what I see in retrospect as the same discriminating judgement that cost me that previously-mentioned job. The one that paid money.

In any case, we caught no bonefish. At night anyway. The number of sharks that came up onto those flats after dark — these were in the Berry Islands — was as impressive as it should have been predictable. I've gotten fairly used to seeing small sharks up on the flats, the usual nurse and lemon varieties running to the occasional four- or five-footer, but these critters were big and they had pointy noses. Or really flat ones. Blacktips and hammerheads. I like a midnight stroll as well as the next guy, and sharks are something I go looking for when I scuba dive, but this moonlight bonefishing seemed a good way to ignite a feeding frenzy without a handy boat to hop into. After a night or two of shark-watching when we were in the boat — they are fascinating, hunting with their noses like sleek black dogs when you toss fresh-cut bait in the shallows — we reverted to the daylight and finished out the trip.

I'm remembering this now, because here is a small shark, bonefish-sized, hunting along beside me as I move up the lagoon. It's about twenty yards away, moving just slightly faster than I am, with its dorsal fin out of the water. If I'd had the Lime Candy or any other bonefish fly on, I'd toss him a cast. They never bite them when I do that, but I don't want to give him the permit fly if he does. Never say never.

Meanwhile I'm envying the little shark its ability to do this from underwater: It's getting hot now, and the wind is still down. I remind myself that this day, especially this midday calm and perfect visibilty, even the heat itself, will be something that I'll treasure in subsequent recollections, the deep winter ones that will have selected out the itchy salt sweat clamming down the back of my clinging shirt. I lift my hat to let some evaporation waft a bit of cooling across my scalp.

If the permit is still in the lagoon, I don't really expect to see it now. The classic permit hunt is done early and late, when the light is down and the wary fish move more freely into skinny water like this. But the permit I saw was moving up into the lagoon, toward where I'm now going, and the tide hasn't yet turned. My bet is that the permit will stay in here, feeding through the whole tide and staying at least until dark. I've got all afternoon to look for it.

Fairly often I've watched local Bahamians walking alone on flats like this or along the shallow edges of channels near settlements, hunting conch or, sometimes, turtles. The old men are certainly hunting conch, moving with the stately precision of blue herons as they traverse an expanse of water on bare feet, with a burlap sack or a plastic pail, always moving in what looks to me from my observed distance like a straight line. They seem to find conchs regularly as they walk, changing neither their demeanor nor their direction of travel when they do, bending fluidly to retrieve the heavy, fluted shells with barely a change in stride before continuing serenely on their prescribed route.

Now I've walked dozens of flats, hunting carefully enough certainly to see conch shells in the water, and I never find them the way these local old men do. Granted I'm not as practiced, but in fact I have tried it, and if I were to go as steadily from one score to the other as they do, I'd be zigzagging all over the flat, picking one up and then scanning right and left for the next before heading that way to get it. Not the old men, the straight walkers of the flats, these conch conjurers who seem to juju them out of nothing at all, conjuring conch shells from the plain bottom as they quietly traverse the shallows.

It would be good, I think to myself, if I could do that here, with a fish. I won't be greedy and try to magic up a permit, but a witchy little bonefish would do just fine right now.

In a straight line, I keep walking. With a warming imagination, I keep looking.

•   •   •

"The bonefish be a peace-lovin' fish, mon," an Exuma guide once explained to Becky and me. "He like to be swimmin' in the calm water so he can lie round and mellow-tate."

Mellowtating is definitely where it's at on the flats, and I may have drifted a bit too deep into it here in the windless lassitude of the lagoon in early afternoon. That wilderness silence I came here to seek has instead found me, secreting itself into all the living separates that combined to form what was, an hour or two ago, a focused fisherman. Now I'm weightless, at once moving through and being an attached part of this place; I haven't had a sequential thought in . . . well, how can I know? And why should I care?

This, I realize with the distant remaining ember of my Western intellect, must be a step toward the sort of extinguishment of all desire that ch'an Buddhism teaches. Mellowtating toward spiritual enlightenment, out on the flats.

No, mon. Uh uh. Wrong thing you said. Mellowtating is enlightenment, mon.

Ah. Yes. Okay . . . Did you say something? Good, mon. Good there. You getting it now.

Once, also on Exuma, up near a fishing settlement called Barre Terre, I was wading a big flat that was new to me, accompanied by a Bahamian named Timothy. He wasn't really a guide, but he was the cousin of one, and he had driven the boat that got me and John Sebright to the back of this flat. It was still and hot like today, and after an hour of watching us fish, Timothy said he needed cigarettes and wandered across the flat toward town, a mile or so away. He came back in forty or forty-five minutes with a cigarette in his mouth and a mixed drink in a glass that he had picked up at the Fisherman's Inn. Ice clinked as he tipped the glass, sipping rum and tonic in the middle of a bonefish flat in the midday heat.

So much for extinction of desire. I can hear the ice clink right now and my daypack is a twenty-minute walk in the other direction. I really should get one of those fanny-packs with the drink holder attached.

Well, let's see. Where am I?

Right. Up here near the small mangroves, now flooded with a foot of fresh tidewater. I'm thinking that this is the definition of a barracuda ambush spot at just about the same moment that I see the long, dark shape motionless against the mangrove roots.

Is that a barracuda? It's about as long as my leg. Fully alerted now, I step quietly closer.

Oh yes. Now I can see the shadow of the fish, lying just an inch or two below it. This is a pretty big 'cuda. I look down to change the permit fly, and I see the long green barracuda fly already attached. What? When did I do that?

Yeah, mon. You be mellowtatin' now . . .

Here is the right fly, properly tied onto the leader. It even has a six-inch heavy-mono shock tippet. It's like coming back to the present on a long drive you've done many times before and realizing that twenty miles have gone by and you don't even remember negotiating a single one of the turns back there. All I can do is shrug. I look back up and the long, dark shape hasn't moved from the mangroves.

I drop the needlefish fly into the water, getting ready to cast, and the barracuda slowly fins out from its hiding place, gliding into open water. Of course it knows I'm here. This will be well into the big fish's second decade, most if not all of it right here in this lagoon; it'll know the territory and all of its vibrations.

But I know the barracuda is aware, not afraid. I don't think of them as ever being afraid. They just go toward things or away from them, driven by a small set of reactions that in some basic Darwinian way has kept them fed, out of harm's way and fabulously prolific; the species is abundant everywhere. Eyeing each other here in the lagoon of clarity, this particular barracuda and I each await the other's next move, sharing in equal measures a tiny slice of space/time, a conflicted set of desires and a mutual distaste for extinction. I roll out a forward cast.

The barracuda flicks its tail, a wide, powerful thing that's bigger than my hand, and coasts farther out into the lagoon as I false cast once, trying to work out enough line to carry the huge green streamer. By the time I get the cast flowing properly, the barracuda has turned and is cruising away from me, forty feet away. It's going to be now or not at all. Pushing hard with my shoulder, I drive the needlefish fly as high and as hard as I can and then let go so the line can shoot out and away. The streamer arcs and then lands with a splash I can hear, right on the fish's tail. Instantly the barracuda jets away.

And almost as instantly the big fish turns right back to see what it was. That's when I start stripping, just a couple of pulls to get its attention. The 'cuda flicks again, back toward the green thing in the water, interested.

I tuck my fly rod under my right arm and grab the fly line with both hands, still twitching the fake needlefish along, watching intently until the barracuda almost imperceptibly accelerates toward it. Then hand over hand I quickly pull on the line, yanking the fly through the water as fast as I can, knowing that this can only last a couple of seconds until I've regained every foot of the cast I made, and watching as the barracuda speeds up, speeds up, and becomes a sudden blur under the surface, and the fly line is jerked from both my hands as the still accelerating barracuda turns with a loud ker-chunk! of violently displaced water right where the fly was and starts running with undiminished speed directly away from me.

I lift the rod and reach for the wildly flapping fly line as it shoots up and out through the stripping guide. The barracuda slows down, thirty feet away from me, content with its catch, completely unaware, just as I regain my grip on the fly line and tighten my hold on it. The fish is still moving away; the line comes taut as I grip it, and I can almost feel the hook bite into the big fish's mouth.

The 'cuda shakes its head, once, twice, pulling

hard on the line and sending shocks all the way through the fly rod to my arm. The hook stays, the leader doesn't part. And then the barracuda leaves.

It tries to leave the lagoon, moving at an astonishing speed, and there's little I can do to stop it. The fly line follows the barracuda, running smoothly out the guides in a couple of seconds and turning yellow without even a bump as the backing seamlessly follows, whining from the reel. A hundred and fifty feet out in the lagoon, the barracuda jumps, a forward-thrusting, flat-trajectory thrash that throws water like a tumbling waterskier. Falling back under, the 'cuda runs on as I lean back against it, barely able to hold the fully-arced fly rod at forty-five degrees. I'll be halfway into the backing very soon.

The fish is off. Instantly and without any shock, as if the leader out there has been sliced with a razor, clean and quick.

With neither an expletive nor a muttering sigh, I begin quietly rewinding. There is no sudden jolt of failure, no instant sense of lost reward, with a cut-off barracuda, not like there is with other fish, the kind you can reasonably expect to land once you've hooked them. With a barracuda, it's too much a part of fishing for them. Every bio-electrical synapse that natural selection has built into the barracuda ends with flashing spark on the sharpened edges of all those teeth; one way or the other, if you choose to connect with them, you're going to get bitten.

Yeah, but, I say to myself as I slowly wind all the slack line back onto the reel. That was a good one.

That really was a good one.

Well, it still is. There's no dishonor in a released fish, and with a barracuda it's a Palm Beach more often than it's not. So 'ere's to you, fishy wuzzy, for you broke me fair and square.

Looking around me, all seems the same as it's been all day, but I have to believe the lagoon is now as collectively traumatized as a deep woods

trout pool through which some Neanderthal has just driven a dirt bike. This makes it easy to decide to walk back to the sand spit and get a drink of water, and to trade in this heavy rod for my lighter bonefish-sized one. After the tarpon and the barracuda, I don't expect any more big-fish events to present themselves; in fact, I'm not sure I even want them. Show me instead a mellowtating bonefish that wants to quietly share some backwater enlightenment.

•   •   •

For the first time since I got here this morning the light in the lagoon is beginning to favor sides, in this case those facing west, toward the sun now halfway down, and with the aging afternoon has come a light, tropical breeze, dry and heated from its invisible passage over the headlands some miles to the southwest. It's a clean wind that carries intermittent small messages from the settlements scattered over the island, picking them up in random and off-chance eddies of heat rising from sun-baked stucco and small backyard fires that never quite go out, from goats walking and paint drying on small boats hauled, from jacaranda trees watered in well-swept courtyards and old conch shells piled behind the government wharf in the main harbor.

Outside the lagoon, just visible over the mangroves, is the white sail of a boat whose hull I can't see as it beats brightly into the freshening breeze out there in the blue water, perhaps a mile offshore. I can tell from the relaxed cut of the sail that it's a local sloop, a working boat still used by some to haul fish traps and to travel to small, uninhabited cays to hunt in their flats and reef tops for conch

and turtle and even to throw a baited hand line for jacks, mutton snapper, grouper and, if it works out, bonefish. They used to throw nets, or string them across the channels, but it's far too deadly on bonefish and it's been outlawed, either by government edict in certain places or by unspoken proscription in others, especially those near the fly fishing resorts.

Some years ago, Becky and I were in a skiff run by David Pinder, Sr., the McLean's Town patriarch of that community which has for several generations provided all the guides for the nearby Deep Water Cay Club. We had run a good number of miles from the club itself, well up onto the Little Bahama Bank, when we came upon a frightened young Bahamian alone in a boat, hiding up in the mangroves. David Sr. apologized first to us for the diversion, and then proceeded to dress down the petrified guy in the other boat, speaking firmly and rapidly in a patois from which I couldn't make out a single word. We then moved on to where David

Sr. wanted us to fish, and when I asked him what had happened back there, he would only say that the young man shouldn't have been there and that he should have known better. That was as much as David Sr. would say about the incident, but I had seen the piled-up green nets in the other boat.

Bonefish are actually fairly good to eat, and the guides I've known have always taken home any accidentally killed ones we've brought to the boat. You wouldn't want to pass over a snapper filet or baked grouper to get at one, but if one of your island friends who knows how to get most of the fine bones out offers to prepare one that was honorably obtained, be sure to accept the dinner invitation. About permit I have no idea, but barracuda is delicious, rendered even more so by the twinge of risk it carries in the form of ciguatera poisoning, a rare but nasty little bug that migrates up the food chain and accumulates, apparently, in the muscle tissue of predator fish, growing in toxicity as the fish grows in size and appetite. Big

'cudas are especially suspect if they come from a reef rather than a flat, but the house odds stack higher with bigger fish from either venue, adding a nice fillip toward any angler's more refined sporting profile. The rewards of catch and release can be for the body too, it seems, but like those for the soul, each one can never be tested against its opposite: each individual fish is either kept or released, is either food obtained and eaten naturally or a meal foregone in the name of prudent restraint.

Catch and release is certainly a religion more easily practiced here on the flats, where your quarry may not trigger your appetite the way it does on a salmon river, but each of us needs to remember that no-kill as a creed provides neither license nor absolution anywhere. Not every fish will survive its encounter with your game, no matter how delicately played, and the choice is not always yours. Even if you didn't intend to kill the fish in question, even — especially — if you intend *never*

to kill one, ever, you still must live with the option that you alone have created by hooking this particular fish: the mindless possibility of death so totally indifferent to your intentions that it sometimes chooses itself spontaneously. Whether you then view the expired fish in your hands as a lamentable tragedy or simply an accidental meal ought to tell you something about how often you should be fishing in the first place.

Fishing is endlessly cautionary and this is certainly its greatest lesson, continually taught and never learned: You can't have it both ways. You really can't.

But you can have something. Especially if you're already standing in the water with a fly rod in your hand. Enough, I decide. Enough of these distractions.

It's time I got back to the bonefish.

●   ●   ●

Some time ago, I just now notice, the tide has turned. The shallow flood that covered all the mangrove roots at the head of the lagoon has now begun to recede, leaving behind, up near the limestone and dry coral edges, a glistening slick of ultrafine sand and marl that you wouldn't actually want to call dry ground. Dotting this wetscape are countless pencil-diameter crab holes, indicating the wealth of the food source here. A source, however, that's in the process of closing itself for the next several hours. The feeding bonefish will be on the move now, heading back out toward the channel and, ultimately, out into deep water until the next high tide.

But they won't be rushing out of the lagoon and I know it. The water level is still good throughout and there are hours left of good light; that which has brought us both in here still holds.

It holds better now, however, out toward the center of the lagoon and that's the direction I'm taking, shuffling slowly and quietly, scanning carefully and with my gear properly rigged and ready. Already I've seen wakes on the far side moving toward the channel and I fully expect to see something nearer to casting distance any time now.

As any fishing day begins to wind down, it's good practice to shut away any looming internal sense that it is. The last thing you want to do is to psychologically compress the remaining time by beginning to measure it. Just keep fishing moment to moment, step to sliding step, right scan to left scan. From fish, if you're lucky, to fish. Like life itself, you want this day to end as more of an annoying surprise than a long, depressing countdown. When the shadows get too long and the light goes off the water, you'll have plenty of time to reminisce; if you do that too soon, you'll just end up recollecting those reminiscences.

And yet it's so hard, isn't it, to fish without resonance. Almost everything you do in angling is repetition. We return to the same rivers, the same flats, the same footprints before they've eroded from wet sand. We cast with the same rod and throw the same line, looping through an arc that

goes out and comes back, goes out and comes back, endlessly recalling itself through the same rhythm and motion with which it promises us something brand new each time we cast it forward. Let me go, it says, just let me go and I'll show you something. Something you've been looking for. Right over here.

Right over here. Really.

There they are. A patch of erratically disturbed water off to my right, a succession of small outgoing wakes running counter to the slight ripples pushed in by the light wind. The surface seems to quiver in place as the opposing frequencies pass through each other. Nervous water, they call it, and the wind alone cannot form it. It has to be fish, every time you see it.

Altering my direction but not my speed, I move to intercept the moving pod of bonefish. I haven't seen them yet, but I know that's what they are. In Florida or South Texas they might be mullet; probably would be in fact, but not here in the Bahamas. And certainly not here in the afternoon of my day alone in this lagoon, my private lagoon whose defined clarity can only show me two things now: light itself or its living cousin, the bonefish.

Or a permit.

With a silver glint, distant, arced and then gone, the permit is here again. I stop, frozen as if I'd just shown myself to an incoming wild turkey at dawn.

And then I relax, keeping my eye on the place where the sickle fin has come up but letting the hunger for it recede from the tension it's formed across my shoulders and down my arms.

No, I decide. I'm not going there. Not now with the bonefish moving closer and the mirage-fin of the permit already losing dimension in my immediate recollection. No, I say to the permit swimming out there and letting it echo to the one in my mind as well. If you want to be part of my lagoon today, then you will have to be a real part of it, not a teasing gestalt glimmering from other places and other times either behind or before me. If you want to be here, I say, then be here.

I turn back, looking for the bonefish. And almost immediately I see them, this time close enough to make out the inch-high ghosting tapers of their tails moving through and with the nervous water. There could be fifty fish in the group, tightly packed and moving together slowly toward the channel.

This is not a situation conducive to an easy hookup. At least not usually. I don't really know why schooled-up bonefish take flies less willingly than they do when hunting alone or in twos and fours, but it's true, especially on an outgoing tide like this. On the other hand, they're usually less spooky; you can get a few tries at them as the school passes by.

What I want to do here, ideally, is to get the fly out in front of them so it appears to the lead fish that they have naturally come across a crab on their route of travel. But there is also danger in doing that, since there almost always is a loose fish swimming apart from the pack; if the fly line lands on the water across his back, he'll be the one to yell "Fire!" in a crowded theater. The whole performance will end then and there, while the overture is still playing.

Still, it's a chance I'll have to take. In this light I don't have eyes practiced enough to detect these accidental picket fish; I can only read the nervous water, select a spot in front and drop the fly there. With one false cast to measure the distance, I do just that.

No pickets. No change in the oncoming ripples. It looks like I'll have five, maybe ten seconds before I should make the little artificial crab move across the bottom in front of them.

I've often wondered what it's like for a real crab, a thumbnail-sized fiddler, say, to be caught out of its hole by a large school of bonefish appearing silently at the blue limit of its vision, coming faster than the crab can possibly run, cruising in like jet-powered anti-gravity killer zeppelins at the

equivalent of utility pole height, shoulder to shoulder and spread out toward infinity in both directions. The only good option, if you still had a functioning mentality after seeing that, would be to freeze immobile. Hunkering down and hoping for the best is, as it turns out, a life-affirming alternative lifestyle for a good number of species besides ourselves.

And yet it's clear that that's not what the actual crabs do: lie low and act like a rock. For if every live crab, or even most of them, did that in the face of a bonefish attack, then bonefish would long ago have naturally selected not to react to the oddity of one of them running away. Many of the small flats crabs can swim if they have to, but you won't get a bonefish to take your artificial version if you pull it through the water column like a black-nosed dace.

So, for reasons known only to the crabs, they run, and frankly it's not my problem. Not, anyway, until the mile-wide spaceships from *Independence Day* show up for real in the night sky over New Hampshire. Meanwhile, knowing that a crab will skitter is an anecdotal but widely-accepted bit of natural history that I think I'll apply in a limited little experiment. Right now.

Strip, strip. Nothing. Strip, strip. Nothing. The fish are definitely right on top of the fly now. Strip, strip, strip.

Nothing.

Quickly pulling in long lengths of line until I'm sure the fly is well out of their path, I pick up, then false cast as I sidestep through the water, trying to keep pace with the slow-moving school. Back in position, I drop the crab fly again in front of the pack. If it doesn't work this time I think I'll risk plopping it down closer, so they can hear it hit the water.

The first time I went redfishing, I went to a lagoon not too different from this one, near Rockport, Texas with Chuck Naiser. You may remember him from a Sage Rod ad that featured him a few years ago; he really is a good guide, and good company, too. Anyway, we were wading with Tom Montgomery in water that wasn't even as deep as this when I saw tailing redfish, rooting for shrimps. I tried to place my Clouser Minnow two feet to the right of them, but I fumbled the cast and it landed maybe ten inches from them. I winced. Nothing happened.

"Got to be closer than that, Ed," drawled Chuck. "You got to let them know it's there."

I tried again, forcing myself to put the fly closer, but I literally couldn't make myself do it. Like an errant wind, the casting synapses I'd developed here in the Bahamas kept at the last second pushing the fly away from the happily feeding redfish. The closest I got in four casts was about six inches. Finally the redfish just put their tails down and disappeared.

"That's no good, Ed," said a disgusted Chuck. "These aren't bonefish. You got to hit them on the head. I mean on the head."

It took two days before I finally muffed a cast so badly that the fly landed right on top of a redfish, which instantly spun, slashed, inhaled the fly and took off.

Another nightmare I now have — though not as sit-sweating-up-in-bed jarring as the giant tarpon version — is a colonization of my Bahamas flats by shoals of transient redfish. You'd have to make a certain species i.d. before each cast: Is that a redfish to hammer or a bonefish to tease? And what if they mingled? I hadn't considered that. This one may now also produce night sweats.

Meanwhile, here in the uninvaded lagoon, my crab fly has once again passed unsampled beneath the moving bonefish. And now they're beginning to get away from me; I don't think I'll be able to get far enough in front of them to make this same sort of presentation again. Now what?

Don't say anything, Chuck. These are bonefish.

I lift and false cast, deciding while the fly is in the air to place it right at the edge of the nervous

water. They may spook, or they may just hear it enough to take an interest.

Ploop. The fly lands. Something happens in the water nearby. The pattern of nervous water is disrupted as shadowy fish jostle and scurry, hunting and dodging, nervous and aggressive. I tuck the fly line against the cork rod handle under the index finger of my right hand and with my left I begin to strip it with short little curls of my wrist.

Strip. Strip. The water's surface above the fly is convoluted, excited. Strip. A bonefish tail splashily breaks the surface, waggling and directed, then disappears. It seems impossible that none of them has picked up the little crab. Strip.

Strip.

I'm beginning to get lightheaded, dizzy; I realize I'm holding my breath. My lungs empty with a sigh I can hear as well as feel. Breathe in. Relax.

Strip.

What is this? They're all over it —

Resistance. A sharp, quick tug. Then nothing.

I pull steadily. Nothing. Oh, come on —

Resistance. Another tug, stronger. I pull back against it, steadily as before. This time the line doesn't want to come back. Without thinking about it I give the line a short, hard strike.

Fish on. The line sizzles out. I lift the fly rod and a seeming acre of water in front of me explodes to a froth as the hooked bonefish runs straight into the panicking school, parting them like Pamplona spectators in front of the charging bulls. It makes me want — almost — to yell out loud. I never even saw the bonefish that took.

This one has power. It runs straight away from me, fast and strong, accelerating, pulling line from the reel so fast that I think I can feel the building heat radiating from the fast-rotating arbor from which a metallic shriek undulates in a rhythmic whine that rises in pitch as the diameter of the disappearing spool of line decreases. It sounds like the reel is throwing a baby's tantrum.

What if it doesn't stop? I ask myself.

Is that possible? How big is this fish?

Big enough, I decide, for me to start palming the reel, a delicate skill that I usually overdo, applying too much friction and breaking off the fish. But my already sweating palm provides all the lubricant I need today; the bonefish stays attached, somewhere far out in the afternoon lagoon, and ultimately, slowly, almost unbelievably, it begins to lose strength. And just as slowly I begin to work against the tiring fish, turning it and starting the long reversal of all that line, out there before me, stretching into the lagoon and all the way past it, to the very connection that brought me here in the first place.

With a slow, calming breath of island-washed air I relax, pulling gently and winding steadily, and begin walking toward the bonefish as I reel it in. I don't know what constitutes halfway, here in the lagoon of clarity, but wherever it is, that's where I want to meet this last bonefish of the day.

•   •   •

My day alone in the lagoon is now pointing toward its own end. Already the tide has drained the back half of the flats here and the sun has angled down far enough that, while the sky has lost none of its apparent brightness, I can no longer cut through the surface sheen with my polaroids. And although there still is a fly rod in my hand, I have, in fact, stopped fishing. The day is too complete, capped with the neat symmetry of beginning and ending bonefish wrapped around a good barracuda and a gift tarpon. Only an avarice that I don't want to own would keep a person hunting after that.

So right now I'm slowly walking across the middle of the lagoon, contentedly heading back toward the sandy spit where I left my green daypack first thing this morning. Only mildly do I regret my decision to drink the Kalik beer at lunch, but it would be just right if I had had the confidence to bring two of them. Perhaps Becky and Roland will have one in the boat with them, on ice and still in the cooler. A good thought, and probably an accurate one. I can wait.

I think. A beer would be good right now, wouldn't it?

Days like this — well, there really aren't any, but nonetheless — I wish I kept a diary, or at least an angling log of some sort. If I did I'm not sure how I would go about it, though. Do you stop in the middle of the day, take away some fishing time and write down an event just after it's happened? No? No, you wouldn't do that. But then what, you write it down later? Okay. Good. Makes better sense. I might do that.

How much later?

I know it's a trick question. That's why I asked it. But we all do have to live with these leaking filters, don't we? The ones that start appearing as soon as we let go of a caught fish or finish a rare glimpse of something. They're an unavoidable aspect of electro-chemical memory, and none of us is without them, say the biophysicists. Or so I think they say: I've got to have filtered that information, too, and the mesh in my science screens seems to get coarser every year.

Where does a memory go when you lose it?

The thing that happened is still there, isn't it? Out in the cone of history and riding the arrow of time just like you and I are? If we alter a remembered event in our minds or if we forget it completely, even if every living thing on earth loses track of it totally, isn't there still a pure record of it, traveling outward at the speed of light, possibly to be picked up and read by some other living thing light years away?

Sure. Of course there is. The arcing flash of this morning's first bonefish, turning with my Lime Candy fly and streaking with its own shadow across the shimmering flat is still an uneroded memory with me, but it's also a bright story speeding outward into the cosmos. It got back to the sun that ignited it in about eight minutes, and now it's hours past that, glimmering toward Orion, the Seven Sisters and beyond.

That was something to see, though, wasn't it? That first bonefish? The stuff, as they say, of dreams.

Well, okay, what about dreams? Fishing dreams, let's say. Does some record of them flicker off, too? And if it does — It must, really. It's electro-chemical, right? Aren't speeding electrons what the universe is all about? — then who's to know out there at the receiving end that that's what this is when it finally gets there? Just a dream. Some guy's fantasy. Not an actual record of something that truly happened, way out there, all those light years away on the edge of that little galaxy, the Milky Way, where recent telemetry indicates the possibility of water on a planet or two.

It doesn't matter, I guess. If they have dreams of their own, they'll know one of ours when it arrives. And if they don't, then there won't be any difference for them; it'll all be real, even the dreams we send.

Hmmm. It'll all be real. I may want to . . .

No, mon. Don't you go that way. That place be too mellow, mon. Water be way too calm over there, mon.

Right. Okay. I can see that. But speaking of calm water, the wind seems to have died.

I stop, look around the lagoon. It's kind of odd for this time of the day, but the wind has laid. All across the shallowing flats the small ripples are dying; the surface is about to go smooth again, just as it was first thing this morning. Out beyond the channel, over the shielding mangroves and coming in from the far horizon, are the building cumulus clouds that I'd have expected to have arrived here on the island by now. Under them will be a warm

wind and a few showers, but it doesn't look like they'll be here very soon.

A nice bonus to the day, I decide. After Becky and Roland get here in the skiff, we should have plenty of time to get back to the dock ahead of any rain. Turning once again to continue my way to the sandy spit and my daypack, I let my eyes drift all the way around the lagoon, taking in the reclaimed calm and the clarifying reflections that its once-again flat surface is now showing.

Far across, in very shallow water broken by rounded mounds of sand appearing with the draining tide, shore birds have begun to arrive, hunting in their own reflections for the same crustaceans the bonefish have now abandoned. Further out toward the middle, a small flurry of underwater action showers the surface; shad maybe, or a small barracuda chasing something. Wondering if any bonefish are still in the lagoon, still feeding, I turn to look at a wider expanse of water. It would be good to know, I decide, if they do feed at this stage of the

tide; I won't always get a midday high like today's.

Something catches my eye out toward the channel. Something moved there, in water still deep enough to give bonefish some confidence. I peer carefully, waiting for another indication.

The sun has angled down fairly low now, far enough so that my polaroids darken the lagoon perhaps a degree or two too much; it's a toss-up whether or not to use them. I lift them, but it's too bright when I do, so back they go.

A small flash, out where the water had moved a minute ago, just as I'm resetting my sunglasses. What was it? Very carefully now I watch, trying not to blink.

And even before it reappears, I know that the permit is back. Like time-lapse photography of a single blade of growing grass, the glinting dorsal rises from underneath the undisturbed surface, waggles just slightly a few inches above it, and then drops back down. It is like time-lapse; I can almost hear the film running in reverse, the old 16mm reel

kind that clicks and hums as it rewinds.

No. It's not the film in my mind. It's Becky and Roland in the skiff, still far away. But coming.

I haven't moved my eyes from the spot. The permit shows again, this time both dorsal and tail. It's definitely feeding. I glance down at my fly rod.

The permit fly is attached. I take a breath and listen.

The boat is still far away. I take another breath and look.

The permit shows again.

Clamping the leader to the rod grip with my right hand, I peel line from the reel as I start in

that direction. If the permit is still there by the time I wade cautiously near enough, it's still going to be a long cast; I don't think I want to risk getting as close as even sixty feet in conditions as shallow and quiet as this.

When I'm a hundred yards away, the permit shows again. I stop, instantly.

The permit is swimming toward me. Even after the fins go down, I can now see the faint surface bulge ahead of the moving fish.

It's coming right at me.

I drop the loops of line in my left hand and begin to work out false casts.

The permit stops, tilts down to feed, splashing slightly with its tail. Now I'm close enough to hear it.

I can also hear the outboard motor, still faint but running at full speed, getting closer. How close will the permit let it come before running for cover? Probably, I decide, until Roland gets to the outside of the channel and suddenly shuts it off.

The permit is under again, and I can't see any bulges in the water. Where is it now? Worried, I let a false cast drop onto the water behind me.

There it is, even closer, maybe seventy yards. Still on line.

The outboard drones on, closer and closer.

I'm going to have to place a cast right now, as far out toward the oncoming permit as I can. Taking in slack from the line out behind me, I carefully accelerate it forward, getting it off the water without any real noise. One false cast to set the direction and then I haul and shoot as best I can, trying to cast above the water, not toward it. The loop unfurls long and straight, as good a cast as I can make, hanging high and straight and then falling quietly onto the still water with a very faint hiss, turning the crab fly at the last second before it would have collapsed, bunching the leader. With a tiny splash, the fly hits and sinks, twenty or thirty feet in front of the permit.

The bulge in the water grows; the permit is accelerating. Toward the fly. I watch it, mesmerized. Is this really going to happen?

Outside, the outboard is getting much closer.

I remind myself to breathe.

The permit reaches the fly. I think. I guess. I don't know. I give the line a small tug, stripping an inch or two.

The permit turns, tips up, turns again. Its tail breaks water.

I strip. No resistance. I strip again. And again. Nothing. The permit is aggressive, hunting hard, waggling its caudal fin as it scours the bottom. I strip again.

What is going on? Can't the permit see the fly? What's it doing, hearing it scrape on the bottom?

The boat is close now. How soon till Roland shuts it down?

I strip, then stop. Strip again. The permit is all over the fly, clearly agitated, almost continually throwing water with its tail. It's only fifty feet away now and I bend down, shrinking my profile from the oncoming fish. Pick up the fly! I strip again, more sharply.

The outboard is a continuous sound now, a sharpening buzz growing louder and louder by the second. So is the strange roar in my ears as the permit gets closer.

And closer. Thirty feet now, two canoe lengths. I can see it perfectly now, closer than any free-swimming permit I've ever been near. Why hasn't it seen me?

I drop to one knee in the water as I strip. Even at this height I can still see the permit, coming, hunting, searching. The outboard sounds like it's right here, in the lagoon.

I put my other knee down and hunker as low as I can, putting the rod tip in the water and pointing it at the fish. The permit still comes. Now the line I'm stripping is thickening: I'm pulling on the weight-forward taper. Soon the Albright knot will be at the rod itself. The oncoming permit will be a leader length away.

Fully prostrate now, bent deep into prayer form, I give the line one more wrist flick even as I know it isn't going to work. The knot ticks against the tip top.

The oncoming outboard shuts off.

Quiet spreads across the lagoon like a disappearing shock wave, extinguishing itself as it goes.

Silence.

The permit stops hunting.

It's over.

All the tension runs out of my body, a literal weight lifted from my back, and I rise up, lifting my head for a glimpse of the permit as it turns; wanting, in the flicker before it leaves me, here in the lagoon of nothing now but clarity, to see, in that one impossible eye, the darkness and the light, the secret and the answer, both together, shining and bright, the memory and the dream.

•　•　•

EPILOGUE

*H*anging like twin silver disks, upright in a shimmer of dispersing blue, the permit hover immobile, watching; they are huge, wide as your outstretched arms, identical, implacable as passing time. Your own breathing rushes hollow, echoed and distant in your ears as you swim vaguely toward them. But they remain away, parallel and alien, each one watching you with a single giant eye. You swim harder, kicking and flailing, your breathing louder and louder, but the permit stay at the same distance, holding just so and staring back, fixed in a liquid universe of radiant water, traversing with you through a world without edges, with no visible bottom and no apparent top, shimmering, sapphire and silent.

Far away now from the flats, you have followed the shadows themselves into the brightness of another day, trailing them as they slipped from the island into the sea, and there, with a tank of air on your back, you have found them, poised in the hundred-foot visibility of the deep cerulean waters outside the reef.

You wonder if they can really be permit, if they aren't something else, something you can't know. Beyond spectral, poised like apparitions in a weightless place, they have presented themselves instead with the quiet gravity of very old life. Hovering in the illuminated density of clear water that envelops them, they barely drift, as if they know that to move is to displace something else, some other part of a world with which they have grown comfortable and to which they now seek no disturbance.

You hover there too, holding out as long as you can, controlling your breathing to conserve the air remaining in your tank and inching closer and ever closer, trying to memorize every detail of the two magnificent fish. You know you will never see anything like them again.

Finally you have to surface; your air is gone. You kick once, displacing yourself gently upward to coast with increasing buoyancy away from the permit, back toward the boat and the people

waiting there for you. You've been down too long and they know it. You know it, too.

But even so you return reluctantly, floating without hurry toward atmosphere and gravity, facing backward to the depths, and the permit disappear as you watch, soundlessly vanishing into the universal blue that slowly takes away their individual shapes, dissolving and reclaiming them.

●　●　●